AND NOBODY GOT HURT!

AND NOBODY GOT HURT!

The World's Weirdest, Wackiest True Sports Stories

BONK!

LEN BERMAN

Illustrated by Kent Gamble

LITTLE, BROWN AND COMPANY

New York ⚓ Boston

To all those blooper-makers over the years—
thanks for the memories . . .
and the laughs —L.B.

To Dana and Ryan —K.G.

Little, Brown and Company

Time Warner Book Group
1271 Avenue of the Americas, New York, NY 10020
Visit our Web site at www.lb-kids.com

First Edition: September 2005

Library of Congress Cataloging-in-Publication Data
Berman, Len.
And nobody got hurt!: 120 of the world's weirdest, wackiest true sports
stories / by Len Berman; illustrated by Kent Gamble.—1st ed.
p. cm.
ISBN 0-316-01029-4
1. Sports—Miscellanea—Juvenile literature. I. Gamble, Kent, ill. II. Title.
GV707.B46 2005
796—dc22
2004029629

10 9 8 7 6 5 4 3 2 1

COM-MO

Printed in the United States of America

The text was set in Galliard, and the display type is Space Toaster.

CONTENTS

AND NOBODY GOT HURT!

WHY DO WE LOVE SPORTS SO MUCH?

I mean, if you aren't a fan, sports are kind of dumb. Take basketball, for instance. People throw a ball into a basket—it's that simple. And just for doing that, players are paid zillions of dollars while millions of fans scream their lungs out. Crazy!

But people love sports. If you wanted to, you could watch sports twenty-four hours a day on television, or you could talk about it all day and all night on those radio shows where they talk sports, sports, and nothing but sports.

You've also probably heard sayings like "Sports is a game of inches" and "That's the way the ball bounces." Well, that's where I come in. Sure, it's neat when your favorite player hits a home run. But it's even neater when the ball bounces off the outfielder's head and *then* goes over the fence. If you're like me, first you laugh, then you wonder what the rule is, and then you tell your buddy about it.

I collect sports bloopers and show them on television in a segment I call "Spanning the World." I show all kinds of wild and wacky, outrageous sports stuff. I've been doing this for nearly twenty years and yet I've never run out of material.

Did you hear about the dwarf who once played major league baseball? Or another big leaguer who ran around the bases *backwards*?

An NFL quarterback once passed the ball to himself! And then there was the Football Hall of Fame star who injured himself during the pregame coin toss!

Did you know there was an NBA basketball player who scored for *both* teams in the same game? Or that there was a basketball game in which the coach ordered one of his players to get down on all fours and bark like a dog?

Have you heard about the NHL hockey game that was canceled because of *fog*? Or the golfer who hit a tee shot that sliced onto a road, bounced off a car, and landed in the cup for a hole in one?

What about the Australian swimming coach who threw a live crocodile into the pool to make his swimmers go faster? You can't make this stuff up!

Even the rules in sports are nuts. For example, what's the deal with lines? In baseball, if a ball hits the foul line it's a fair ball. But in football, if you step on the line you're out of bounds. In tennis, if a ball hits the line it's good. But in basketball, dribble on the line and it's a turnover. Make up your mind, already!

Sometimes sports can be dumb and sometimes sports can be goofy, but no matter what we still LOVE 'em! In the following pages, you'll see why.

BASEBALL

For it's one, two, three strikes, you're out,
At the old ball game!

Sounds so simple, doesn't it? Three strikes, you're out. Three outs per inning. But in baseball it's not quite that simple. Anything can happen . . . and it usually does.

I've seen a pitched ball bounce and wind up in the umpire's shirt pocket. I've seen a ground ball bounce down the first baseman's shirt. And I've seen a batted ball hit so hard it got stuck in the fielder's glove.

I've seen a shortstop tag the umpire by mistake at second base. And there was an outfielder who didn't bother fielding a base hit—when the ball came to him he just kicked it back to the infield!

Foul balls do the craziest things. I've seen one go on a fly right into a garbage can in the stands. Another foul ball went into the press box and smashed a television set—the ball wound up inside the TV!

I've seen two players catch the same ball at once. And I've seen two runners on a base at the same time.

Balls, bats, players, and fans can all take funny bounces. That's what this chapter is all about. So just pull up a chair, *buy me some peanuts and Cracker Jack*, and enjoy.

Play ball!

In May 1993 at the old Cleveland Municipal Stadium, the Indians' Carlos Martinez hit a long fly ball to right. Jose Canseco was the right fielder that day for the Texas Rangers. But as he put his glove up to catch the ball it hit him squarely on top of his head and bounced over the wall for a home run!

Sportscasters everywhere thought they were clever when they said "It's about time Canseco used his head!"

In May 1998, in a minor league baseball game in Shreveport, Louisiana, pitcher Randy Phillips was hit in the head by a hard-line drive. He dropped to the pitcher's mound face first, but the

ball popped high into the air and was caught on the fly by the first baseman for an out.

Phillips received fourteen stitches, but he didn't miss his next start. Now that's a hardheaded pitcher!

On June 23, 1963, outfielder Jimmy Piersall of the New York Mets hit the 100th home run of his major league career. He celebrated by running around the bases *backwards.*

The pitcher, Dallas Green of the Philadelphia Phillies, didn't think it was funny. Nor did the Mets' manager—he handed Jimmy his walking papers a few days later.

In June 1999, the Yankees were hosting the Mets at Yankee Stadium. Rey Ordonez of the Mets hit the ball hard—right back to the mound. Orlando Hernandez, the Yankee pitcher known as El Duque, made a backhand grab on one bounce. But the ball was hit so hard he couldn't get it out of his glove.

What did El Duque do? He threw the glove—with the ball still inside it—over to first for the out. And it counted!

Hernandez isn't the only pitcher with an unusual fielding style. In June 1996 at Shea Stadium, Edgar Renteria of the Florida Marlins hit a comebacker to the mound. Mets pitcher Pete Harnisch stuck out his rear end and "butted" the ball over to his third baseman who threw to first for the out.

Harnisch turned out to be a real buttinsky, huh?

Can a ball hit the bat twice on the same play?

In July 2000, Todd Hollandsworth was batting for the Los Angeles Dodgers against the Colorado Rockies. But when he hit the ball his bat shattered, and the ball grounded toward second base while half of the bat flew toward first. Rockies second baseman Todd Walker fielded the ball, but his off-balance throw to first bounced in the dirt. Actually, it didn't hit the dirt—it bounced off the broken part of the bat and rolled away. Hollandsworth was safe at first!

In April 1992, Kirk Gibson was playing for the Pittsburgh Pirates. He only appeared in sixteen games that season, but one of them was unique.

The Pirates were playing the Chicago Cubs at Wrigley. Gibson was the base runner at first when his manager called for a hit-and-run. As the pitcher began his delivery, Gibson took off for second, but his batting helmet came off. And wouldn't you know it . . . the batted ball, which would have been a single to right, hit Gibson's helmet that was lying on the ground.

The ball ricocheted to Cubs second baseman Ryne Sandberg. Gibson, thinking the ball was in right field, rounded second and headed for third. He was caught in a rundown and easily tagged out. His batting helmet is what got him out!

Was he the original Wallbanger?

During a May 1991 game at Civic Stadium in Portland, Oregon, outfielder Rodney McCray ran through a plywood fence in right field while trying to catch a fly ball.

McCray was not hurt. In fact, he became famous for this play as newscasts all across the country showed it over and over.

In August 1987, Cleveland fans gathered to watch the Indians' minor league team, the Williamsport Bills, battle the Reading Phillies.

In the fifth inning, with a Reading runner on third, Bills catcher Dave Bresnahan called time-out. He told the home plate umpire something was wrong with his catcher's mitt and went to the dugout to retrieve another one. Only . . . his new mitt contained a potato! After catching the next pitch, Bresnahan rifled the potato over the head of the third baseman into left field. The runner jogged home, thinking the ball was thrown away and he was going to score easily. But Dave had a surprise—he still had the ball, and he tagged the runner out.

The Bills players thought it was funny, but the umpire wasn't amused. He allowed the run to score. The Bills manager didn't find it funny either. He removed Dave from the game and fined him fifty dollars. The next day, the team released Bresnahan, and his baseball career was over.

In a July 1999 Texas League baseball game in Midland, Texas, a batter bunted down the first base line. As the ball approached the foul line, catcher Yorvit Torrealba dropped to the ground and blew the baseball foul. And the umps allowed it!

On July 31, 1990, Nolan Ryan and the Texas Rangers defeated the Milwaukee Brewers, 11–3, for Ryan's three hundredth career victory. Only twenty-one pitchers in major league history have won that many.

While Ryan was pitching the game in Milwaukee, thousands of his fans gathered in the Rangers stadium in Texas to watch the game on the scoreboard and cheer him on. They were there to watch television. . . . So why did many of the fans bring their gloves? I'm still trying to figure that out.

At a South Atlantic League minor league game on July 14, 2003, the Charleston RiverDogs in South Carolina staged Silent Night at the ballpark. Everyone came, but nobody cheered. Many fans in the crowd of 2,924 wore duct tape across their mouths and held up signs that read YEAH or BOO, depending on what was happening. And when the home team scored a run, all you heard were teammates clapping in the dugout.

They broke the record for the quietest baseball game in history, set back in 1909 by the New York Highlanders (later the Yankees) and the Jersey

City Skeeters. Back then, the laws in New Jersey required fans to keep quiet on Sundays.

In 2002, this same Charleston club held Nobody Night, which set the record for lowest attendance in a professional baseball game. How'd they do that? They locked the gates of the ballpark! No fans could get in. Zero.

After the fifth inning, the game was official—the record was theirs!— so they opened the gates and allowed fans to enter for the rest of the game.

Who would come up with such promotions? The owner of the RiverDogs was Mike Veeck—he's the son of Bill Veeck, the original "P.T. Barnum of baseball" and the man who sent a dwarf up to bat.

On August 19, 1951, the St. Louis Browns were stuck in last place. Attendance was so bad that owner Bill Veeck decided to liven things up. In the bottom of the first inning, the Browns's manager sent a pinch hitter up to the plate. Eddie Gaedel was only 3 feet 7 inches tall, and he weighed just sixty-five pounds. Wearing the number 1/8 on his uniform, Gaedel crouched low at the plate, giving him a strike zone of less than two inches.

Eddie walked on four pitches and trotted down to first base, where he was replaced by a pinch runner and left the game to a standing ovation. Two days later, the American League barred dwarfs from appearing in any more games.

During the 1980s there was a performer at minor league ballparks known as Captain Dynamite. His act was rather simple—he would place a large box out behind second base and line it with dynamite; then he'd climb inside. The crowd would count down, "10 . . . 9 . . . 8 . . . " and then the Captain would blow himself up.

Surprisingly, he was never hurt. I once tracked down Captain Dynamite and he was all in one piece. He *was* a little hard of hearing, though.

In August 1983, the New York Yankees were in Toronto to play the Blue Jays. As outfielders do before each inning, Yankee Dave Winfield was warming up his arm by playing catch with the batboy. Unfortunately, one of his throws hit a sea gull and killed it. After the game, Winfield was arrested by the Toronto police and charged with cruelty to animals! The next day the local prosecutor dropped the charges.

In March 2001, Arizona Diamondbacks pitcher Randy Johnson accidentally killed a low-flying dove that happened to be crossing home plate at the same time as one of his 100 mph fastballs.

In July 1996, the Detroit Tigers were playing in Milwaukee. With a runner on base, Mike Potts of the Brewers threw a curveball to Brad Ausmus of the Tigers. The pitch bounced in front of home plate, but Ausmus swung anyway and hit the ball into right field. A run scored.

Did it count? Absolutely! A bounce-bloop run batted in for Brad Ausmus!

Brad Ausmus wasn't so lucky the next time he found himself in the middle of a play with a funny bounce.

In July 1998, the White Sox were visiting the Houston Astros. Frank Thomas of the Sox was at the plate, with teammate Ray Durham on third. Butch Henry was on the mound for Houston when his pitch bounced away from catcher Brad Ausmus. Ausmus turned around and around, but he couldn't find the baseball. That's because the ball somehow went into the umpire's shirt pocket! And while Ausmus was still searching for the ball, Durham scampered home.

Actually, Durham would have been entitled to home plate even if Ausmus had found the ball. The rules state that if a ball gets caught in the umpire's equipment, the runner is allowed to advance one base.

In June 2000, the Detroit Tigers were hosting the New York Yankees. In the bottom of the first, there was a foul ball down the right field line, and a fan reached over the railing and gloved the ball. Later in that same inning, it happened again—the same fan caught another foul ball to right. Then in the eighth inning, Chuck Knoblauch of the Yankees lifted a foul ball and—you guessed it—this same fan caught it on the fly.

Can you believe one guy was able to catch three foul balls in one game? Maybe it's because he brought three kids to the game!

In September 1992, David Hulse of the Texas Rangers was batting against the California Angels. Hulse hit a line drive foul directly into the Angels dugout. Then he did it a second time. And a third time. So all the Angels moved down to one side of the dugout, huddling together for safety. Some of them even waved white towels as if to say, "We surrender."

On the next pitch, Hulse fouled it right into the part of the dugout where all the Angels had just been seated. Too bad Hulse didn't have the same accuracy when it came to hitting the ball fair. He grounded out to shortstop.

Baseball has supermen just like comic books. On July 20, 1973, knuckleballer Wilbur Wood pitched *both* games of a doubleheader against the New York Yankees. . . . But he also lost both, 12–2 and 7–0.

On July 10, 1932, a thirty-four year old pitcher named Ed Rommel tossed the game of his life. Having already pitched the two previous days, Rommel threw batting practice. But when the starting pitcher was knocked out after the first inning, Rommel came in and pitched seventeen innings of relief. That's almost two full games! And even though Rommel gave up 33 hits, 8 walks, and 14 runs, his Philadelphia Athletics eventually won the game!

On September 9, 1965, Bert Campaneris played all nine positions in the field for the Kansas City

Athletics. Usually the shortstop, Bert played one inning at each position, including the full eighth inning as a pitcher, where he gave up just one run.

Cesar Tovar of the Minnesota Twins matched this feat on September 22, 1968. He began by pitching a scoreless first inning—by coincidence retiring Bert Campaneris as the first batter!

Joel Youngblood is the only major league baseball player to get two hits for two different teams on the same day—and he did it in two cities!

When he woke up on August 2, 1982, Youngblood was an outfielder for the New York Mets. In an afternoon game against the Chicago Cubs at Wrigley he had a two-run single in the third inning. But in the fourth the Mets told him he had been traded to the Montreal Expos. So Joel packed his bags and headed to Philadelphia, where the Expos were playing that night. He arrived during the third inning, donned his new uniform, and got a hit in that game as well!

The Trenton Thunder, a New York Yankees minor league baseball club in Trenton, New Jersey, has a bat dog who runs out to home plate and re-trieves the bats left by Trenton hitters. Chase, a golden retriever, also carries a basket filled with bottles of chilled water. He delivers them to the umpires before the sixth inning.

I guess bat dogs are a lot cheaper than bat boys—they get paid with a pat on the head or a yummy treat!

At San Quentin State Prison in California they have a baseball team made up of inmates. When outside teams come to play, fellow inmates fill the stands. For obvious reasons, the San Quentin team doesn't get to play any "away" games.

In May 1997, Bip Roberts of the Kansas City Royals became a human rain delay. He stood at the plate facing Detroit Tigers pitcher Felipe Lira and fouled off pitch after pitch after pitch—fourteen fouls in all. You'd have thought they would run out of balls.

Roberts batted for a major league record—fourteen minutes. This at bat included a called strike, two pitchouts, and nine throws to first to hold the runner. Was it worth the wait? Roberts eventually grounded out to second base.

Seven years later, Alex Cora of the Los Angeles Dodgers outdid Roberts. In a game at Dodger stadium in May 2004, Cora had a 2–2 count against Chicago Cubs pitcher Matt Clement. And the count stayed the same for almost twelve minutes as Cora fouled off pitch after pitch. On the eighteenth pitch, thirteen minutes and fifteen seconds after his at bat began, Cora finally hit the ball in fair territory—for a two-run homer! Guess he was waiting for his pitch.

What's the record for most pitches in one at bat in the major leagues? On June 26, 1998, Bartolo Colon of the Cleveland Indians threw twenty pitches to Ricky Gutierrez of the Houston Astros—strike, strike, foul, ball, foul, ball, foul, foul, foul, foul, foul, foul, ball, foul, foul, foul, foul, foul, foul, strikeout!

Oops! In the fourth inning of an August 2000 game at Shea Stadium, the San Francisco Giants had runners on second and third. The batter hit a routine fly ball to left and Mets left fielder Benny Agbayani caught it. Thinking it was the third out, Benny handed the ball to a seven-year-old boy in the stands. But it was only the second out. . . .

When he realized what he'd done, Benny grabbed the ball out of the boy's hand and threw home, but two runs came in on the play when only one should have scored. Luckily for Benny, the Mets still won the game, 3–2.

Some people think every baseball player makes millions of dollars. Not true, especially in the minor leagues. When playing at home, if a player on the El Paso Diablos hits a home run, fans drop dollar bills in a batting helmet for the player to keep! Fans also stick dollar bills in the screen behind home plate. The player walks along plucking the dollars out.

Hit a homer in El Paso and you really become the "cleanup hitter!"

At a 1985 minor league baseball game in Clearwater, Florida, organist Wilbur Snapp didn't like an umpire's call at first base. . . . So he played "Three Blind Mice" on his organ. The umpires were not amused. They proceeded to throw the organist out of the game!

In May 2004, superstar Sammy Sosa injured himself when he sneezed twice while bent over in the Chicago clubhouse, sending his back into spasms and taking him out of the Cubs lineup.

But if you think sneezing is a strange way to injure yourself, Hall of Fame third baseman Wade

Boggs once missed a week after injuring himself while pulling on a pair of cowboy boots. And legendary Atlanta Braves pitcher John Smoltz once scalded his chest while ironing a shirt—one that he was actually wearing!

What are the strangest on-the-field injuries?

St. Louis Cardinals star base stealer Vince Coleman missed the 1985 World Series after he was run over by a tarp. Vince was stretching before Game Four of the National League playoffs when someone on the grounds crew activated a machine that automatically rolls up the 120-foot tarpaulin which covers the infield during pregame warm-ups and rain delays. Unfortunately, he didn't see that Coleman was standing near the tarp. The heavy cylinder rolled over his leg, badly bruising him and chipping a bone in his left knee. Vince was carried off the field on a stretcher. "That tarp was a real man-eater," Coleman joked afterward.

Tagg Bozied, star first baseman for the Portland Beavers minor league club, hit a grand slam in the bottom of the ninth for a come-from-behind 8–5 win in July 2004. As he rounded third base he saw his teammates gathered around home plate to celebrate. When Bozied reached the plate he jumped for joy, the way big leaguers do . . . and blacked out. He'd ruptured a tendon in his left knee and was out for the rest of the season. "To go from hitting a walk off home run to being wheeled off the field in an ambulance, it's unbelievable," Bozied said.

But perhaps the weirdest baseball injury of all time happened to pitcher Clarence "Climax" Blethen, a thirty-year-old rookie for the 1923 Boston Red Sox. Clarence thought he'd look tougher if he took out his false teeth when he pitched, so he kept them in his back pocket. During a game in September, Blethen got on base but forgot to put his teeth back in. So when he slid into second attempting to break up a double play, Clarence bit himself in the butt.

Early in a June 2001 game in Pittsburgh, Pirates manager Lloyd McClendon had protested a couple of calls made by the first base umpire. But when he came out of the dugout in the seventh inning to argue a close play, the umpire ejected him.

So McClendon picked up the first base bag and took it with him. He's got to be the first *manager* to ever steal first!

Did you hear the one about the runner on second who tried to steal first?

It happened on August 13, 1902. In the sixth inning of a game between the Philadelphia Athletics and the Detroit Tigers, Harry Davis of the A's was on first and Dave Fultz was on third. Davis and Fultz tried a delayed double steal— Davis took off for second, trying to draw a throw that would allow the runner on third to score. But Davis's steal didn't draw a throw from the Tigers, and Fultz had to remain at third.

On the next pitch Davis headed back to first base! Again, there was no throw from the stunned Tigers catcher. So Davis stole second *again*, and this time the frustrated catcher tried to nail him. Fultz was able to steal home and Davis was safe at second. Was this a double steal or a quadruple steal?

EXTRA INNINGS

A fair ball has never been hit clear out of Yankee Stadium.

In May 1882, umpire James Hickey called out Cleveland outfielder John Richmond for going outside the base path while running to first base on a *walk*.

In a 1917 World Series game, Chicago White Sox pitcher Red Faber tried to steal third base even though a teammate was already standing there.

In the seventh inning of a 1959 game, the Chicago White Sox scored 11 runs on just 1 base hit . . . along with 10 walks, 3 errors, and one hit batter.

Minor leaguer John Neves wore a backward 7 as his uniform number because Neves is "seven" spelled backwards. And in 1978, Al Oliver wore the number 0 on his Texas Rangers uniform.

The first grand slam of Sammy Sosa's career was his 246th career homer. So when did Sammy hit his second grand slam? The next day.

The oldest man to hit a major-league home run is 46-year-old Jack Quinn, a pitcher for the 1930 Philadelphia Athletics.

Tony Cloninger, a pitcher for the Milwaukee Braves, hit two grand slams in one game on July 3, 1966.

In his first major league at bat, pitcher Hoyt Wilhelm hit a home run. It was his only home run in a 21-year career.

During his record 56-game hitting streak in 1941, Joe DiMaggio hit 56 singles and scored 56 runs.

Chicago Cubs' Jim "Hippo" Vaughn and Cincinnati Reds' Fred Toney pitched the only double no-hitter in major-league history on May 2, 1917. In the tenth inning, Vaughn gave up 2 hits and a run and lost the game.

FOOTBALL

Who came up with this sport, you might ask? Nobody is quite sure.

There's some evidence that the Chinese played a game similar to football back in 200 B.C.! That must have been interesting. I'm guessing they didn't have uniforms, cheerleaders, or goalposts. But who really knows?

Let's start with the obvious. Football is one of the sports in which the ball isn't round. So footballs just don't roll along the ground, as in other sports. At times, chasing a loose football resembles a greased watermelon contest.

I've seen guys run the wrong way for "touchdowns" and I've seen them spike the ball in celebration *before* they've reached the end zone.

Players do all kinds of things in the end zone after scoring touchdowns. Most of them dance, but one guy grabbed a cell phone *in the end zone* to call home and say, "Look at me!"

And they don't have rainouts in football. I've seen a game played during a monsoon where pieces of equipment went floating down the field!

Of course, football fans do plenty of wacky things as well . . . like running on the field trying to steal the football. Not real bright, especially when a three-hundred-pound lineman smashes them into the ground.

So let's put on the pads and get ready for the kickoff to some fantastic football follies.

On the first play of an October 1997 Wichita, Kansas, high school game, the quarterback suddenly stopped barking signals and yelled out that he had the wrong football. He said it wasn't the game ball, it was a practice ball. His coach shouted, "Hey, I've got the right ball over here."

The quarterback started walking over to his coach. But as he walked past the line of scrimmage, the quarterback took off and started running full speed with the "wrong" ball. He went all the way for a touchdown—and it counted!

Is this coach crazy? With just seven seconds left in a football game in Mississippi, Tishomingo High School was beating Faulkner High, 16–14.

But Coach Dave Herbert knew that Tishomingo needed to win the game by four or more points to qualify for the state play-offs. So he ordered his quarterback—who was also his son—to turn and run into his own end zone for a safety.

His astonished quarterback did as he was told and after the safety the game was tied, 16–16. Then came overtime, and Tishomingo won the game 22–16—enough to send Coach Herbert's team to the state playoffs!

Turk Edwards is now a member of the Pro Football Hall of Fame, but he left the game after one of the goofiest injuries in the history of sports.

As captain of his Washington Redskins team, Edwards would meet the referee and the opposing captain in the center of the field before each game for the coin toss to decide who would receive the opening kickoff. Early in the 1940 season, Edwards turned to go back to the sidelines after a coin toss, and his cleats caught in the turf. He was carried off the field with a badly injured left knee. Amazingly, he never recovered, and his twelve-year career was over!

During a September 2000 game at Oregon State, a possum wandered onto the field. Then he started running down the field. . . .

The television play-by-play from Tom Kelly and Craig Fertig was terrific: "He's just over the 50 . . . at the 45, nobody going after him. He's on a breakaway at the 40 . . . the 35. To the cheers of 41,000, he's at the 25. He's a straight-line runner, doesn't have many moves. He doesn't need them.

Do you think anyone's going after him? Look at the crowd, the crowd's going crazy! He's breaking to the outside, smells the goal line. Touchdown!"

That day, Oregon State beat USC for the first time in thirty-three years. It must have been that good-luck possum!

Can you pass the ball to yourself?

In 1959, the Cleveland Browns were playing the Chicago Cardinals. Browns quarterback Milt Plum tried to pass, but a Chicago defender blocked the throw. Fortunately, the ball bounced back to Plum, who caught it and ran for a twenty-yard gain.

Who's got the ball?

During a Kentucky vs. Tennessee college football game, a runner fumbled the ball near the Kentucky bench. As people on the sidelines tried to get out of the way, a large box filled with footballs was knocked over and eight of them rolled onto the field. Naturally, players from both teams fought to recover all of the balls. When the play was over, the referee couldn't tell which ball was the official game ball.

He eventually decided to give possession to Tennessee. His reasoning? Well, the Tennessee players had five of the nine footballs, while the Kentucky players got only four!

In October 1989, the folks at Portland State University in Oregon had an unusual idea for a football game. Each fan received a card that said RUN and another that said PASS. Each fan held up one of the cards. The majority ruled, and the offense ran the play the fans selected.

It didn't work very well. I guess Portland State was playing a team whose defense could read!

In an October 1990 college football game in Westchester, New York, Iona kicker Eric Menocal went back to punt. Unfortunately, the snap hit the ground and then Menocal bobbled it. When he finally kicked the football it went straight up in the air. The punt came down behind the line of scrimmage and teammate Tom Kelleher caught it on a fly. He started running and made it into the end zone for a touchdown. And it counted!

Football

What was the shortest punt ever?

In a 1965 Massachusetts game against Amherst College, Tufts University kicker Jay Estabrook was asked to punt. Kicking into a 25 mph wind, the ball blew right back at him. Estabrook caught his own punt and was tackled for a four-yard loss.

What's the weirdest touchdown in football history?

In December 2000, Central College of Iowa was playing football at Linfield College in McMinnville, Oregon. The game went into overtime and Linfield kicked a field goal to lead by three points. In the last few seconds of the overtime period, Central College lined up to kick a field goal which would have tied the game. When Linfield blocked the kick, all of the players on the Linfield sidelines went running onto the field to celebrate what they thought was a win. The crowd of 2,500 happy Linfield fans was jumping for joy. But while they were rejoicing, a Central player picked up the loose ball and ran for the winning touchdown!

• • •

During the final moments of a November 20, 1982 game, Stanford University scored a touchdown to take the lead over archrival University of California at Berkeley, 20–19. With just seconds left to play, Stanford kicked off. The ball was caught by a Cal player named Kevin Moen. As he was about to be tackled, Moen threw a lateral pass to a teammate. By this time the clock had run out, but in football the game is not over until the final play is complete. So, to keep the play alive, Cal players continued to lateral the ball again and again to avoid being tackled.

Meanwhile, thinking the game was over, the Stanford band marched onto the field. By this time, Kevin Moen had retrieved the ball. He darted among the surprised band members and even ran over a trombone player in the end zone. Moen scored the winning touchdown, one of the craziest ever, winning the game for California 25–20!

What about the trombone player? Fortunately, nobody got hurt!

In the closing seconds of a December 2002 Washington State Championship semifinal game, Lynden Christian High School had the ball and

was leading Elma High by a score of 19–14. The quarterback took the snap and intentionally ran back toward his own end zone to run out the clock. Time ran out as the Lynden quarterback crossed the goal line, so he just dropped the ball on the turf. He thought the game was over.

Wrong. An Elma player picked up the ball that was on the ground and it was the winning touchdown! The final score—Elma 20, Lynden Christian 19.

In November 2002, Louisiana State University was playing at the University of Kentucky. With just two seconds to go and the home team leading 30–27, the Kentucky players gave Coach Guy Morriss the traditional Gatorade shower on the sidelines. Students were poised to tear down the goalposts. But then LSU pulled the old Hail Mary play—a last second desperation heave into the end zone while the quarterback and the rest of his team pray that they complete it.

LSU's prayers were answered and they won the game 33–30. As for Kentucky—oops!

• • •

It was September 11, 1995, and the Chicago Bears were playing the Green Bay Packers at Soldier Field, Chicago. In the third quarter, Kevin Butler kicked an extra point for Chicago, and Bears fan Mike Pantazis leaped from his seat in the end zone, right above one of the tunnels leading to the exits. Mike timed his jump perfectly, caught the ball in midair, and fell *twenty feet* to the concrete below. And he didn't get hurt!

The game was being broadcast on *Monday Night Football,* and 42 million people watched the slow-motion replay. Later, Mike was interviewed on the sidelines, where he said that his high school football coach always claimed he had good hands.

On Thanksgiving Day 1998, the Detroit Lions and Pittsburgh Steelers were getting ready for overtime. Back judge Phil Luckett tossed the coin to see who would get the ball first, and Jerome Bettis of the Steelers called "tails." Somehow, Luckett thought Bettis had called "heads," and when the coin landed on tails he awarded the ball to Detroit, even though Pittsburgh had really won the toss.

The Lions then marched down the field and kicked the winning field goal.

On October 20, 2002, during a New Orleans Saints game against the San Francisco 49ers, a fan ran onto the field and joined the 49ers huddle. He just stood there, pen in hand, offering *his* autograph to the San Francisco players.

They declined his invitation, and he was arrested for trespassing.

In September 1996, Ohio State hosted Pittsburgh in college football and the Buckeyes won 72–0.

How bad was it? Well, for one punt return, Ohio State had only eight men on the field. But with only seven of his teammates to block eleven Pitt Panthers, David Boston caught the punt and raced sixty six yards for a touchdown!

You think that was a lopsided game?

Back in 1916, the powerful Georgia Tech team was coached by the legendary John Heisman, for whom the Heisman Trophy is named. The

Heisman Trophy is awarded each year to the most outstanding college football player in the country.

On October 7th, Georgia Tech defeated little Cumberland University by a score of 222–0. This game was so one-sided that Tech set the record for most touchdowns in a game—thirty-two—and Cumberland never even managed a first down. In fact, *neither* team made a first down—Tech scored every time it got the ball!

Things got so bad that late in the game a Cumberland runner fumbled the ball. As it rolled toward his teammate B. F. Paty, the fumbler shouted, "Pick it up!" and Paty replied, "Pick it up yourself—you dropped it!"

O.J. McLintock was a terrific high school quarterback from Round Rock, Texas. In a game in September 1998, McLintock took the ball himself and went weaving through the entire defense. They couldn't get hold of him. But they did somehow manage to grab the back of his athletic supporter. In fact, they were able to pull it completely out of his pants. And as they did the fabric began to unravel like a ball of string.

44

O.J. went all the way for the touchdown, and all that the defense had to show for their efforts were the threads of his jock strap!

In a November 1989 football game in Iowa, the Graceland College team was kicking for an extra point after a touchdown. The ball bounced off the upright and came directly back to the player who'd held the ball for the kicker. He took the ball and ran it into the end zone. Graceland thought they'd scored two points. They were wrong; the play did not count, but the holder should have gotten extra points for creativity!

In a July 1991 Canadian Football League game in Edmonton, punt returner Gizmo Williams—who had already returned one punt for a touchdown—was well on his way to returning another. He broke into the clear, and as Gizmo neared the end zone the TV announcer yelled, "Touchdown!"

There was one problem—Gizmo thought he'd crossed the goal line when he dropped the ball on the ground. Turned out he was at the five-yard line. Oops. No touchdown—it was a turnover instead!

The same thing happened in a July 1992 NFL exhibition game. Standing on the 42-yard line, New York Jets quarterback Browning Nagle threw a pass to wide receiver Rob Carpenter. Carpenter caught the ball on the 14 and had an open field to the end zone. But Carpenter celebrated too early—he spiked the ball at the two-yard line! Only, in this case, the confused referee signaled touchdown . . . and it counted!

In December 1995, Bluefield was playing Musselman in the West Virginia High School Championship. When the game began, Musselman kicked off and the ball rolled dead on the two-yard line. But nobody on the Bluefield team picked it up. The ball was just lying there on the field—a live ball!

A Musselman player grabbed it and it was their ball on the Bluefield two-yard line! Musselman went on to win the state's AA Championship.

In December 1994, the Plano East High School football team trailed John Tyler High School 41–17 in a Texas state semifinal game. Plano roared back to score twenty-seven straight points and took a 44–42 lead with just seconds left to go. All they had to do was kick off and tackle the receiver, and the game was over.

TV announcer Mike Zoffuto made the following call as Tyler kickoff returner Roderick Dunn began running up the field: "No . . . Oh, no! No!! Oh my gosh!! No!!! Come on!! No, no! Gosh . . . I'm sick, I'm gonna throw up."

If you haven't guessed by now, Dunn returned the kick ninety-three yards for a touchdown, and Tyler won the game 48–44.

OVERTIME

Washington Redskins kicker Mark Moseley, who once made a record 23 consecutive field goals, wore five pairs of socks on his kicking foot.

What are the fewest yards gained rushing in an NFL game? A minus 53 by the Detroit Lions in 1943. And the fewest yards gained passing in a game? Also a minus 53, by the Denver Broncos in 1967.

On October 9, 1960, the Dallas Cowboys were just two inches from the goal line. Knowing that everyone expected a run, quarterback Eddie LeBaron stepped back and threw a pass to his left end—touchdown!

In his first college game, LSU receiver Carlos Carson caught five passes, all for touchdowns.

Prairie View A&M University in Texas, a Division I-AA school, lost a record eighty consecutive football games, from November 1989 until September 1998.

Minnesota Vikings kicker Gary Anderson set the NFL record in 1998 for most points after touchdown made in a season, 59, without a miss. He also went 35 for 35 on field-goal attempts during the regular season.

Cal Hubbard is the only man in both the Baseball and Pro Football Halls of Fame. He was a star NFL lineman from 1927–33 and 1935–36 and an American League umpire from 1936–51.

The longest field goal in the NFL is 63 yards, but the longest field goal ever is by a high school player—68 yards, by Dirk Borgognone in Reno, Nevada, in 1985.

Deion Sanders, an All-American defensive back for Florida State University, was drafted by the Atlanta Falcons. He was also drafted by the New York Yankees as an outfielder. On September 5, 1989, Deion hit his first home run in the major leagues. And five days later he scored his first NFL touchdown for the Falcons with a 68-yard punt return!

BASKETBALL

Many people consider basketball to be the only true American sport. It was invented in America—Springfield, Massachusetts, to be exact. The inventor was Dr. James Naismith—a Canadian.

That means that the only true "American" game was invented by someone from another country. Maybe that's why the basketball often takes such funny bounces.

Naismith invented basketball in 1891 using a soccer ball and two peach baskets. Every time somebody scored, a guy had to climb a ladder to retrieve the ball. It took ten whole years to realize they should cut out the bottom of the basket!

I've seen all kinds of crazy things at basketball games. One ball bounced off a player's head and into the basket. I've seen a player bounce the ball hard off the court, high in the air . . . and into the basket!

I've seen a player dribbling down the court on a fast break and the opposing coach run out and block him!

And fans? Some of them pay a great deal of money to sit in the first row. So what happens—huge players run over them at full speed, spilling the fan's popcorn or soda all over them.

Get ready to "hoop it up" for some of the wildest and craziest moments in basketball.

In the March 17, 1998 Idaho Class A-3 state high school championship game, Kimberly High took a two point lead with just 2.9 seconds to go. The team's fans were going crazy, hugging and screaming, thinking they'd won. Then Mike Christensen, a senior at tiny Declo High, took the inbounds pass, dribbled to the free throw line, and flung the ball seventy-five feet, nearly the entire length of the court and . . . it went in! Mike won the championship for Declo, 72–71.

Later, Mike said, "It was just like in the movies. Everything seemed to go totally quiet and the ball just kind of hung in slow motion."

A few days later Declo High held a pep rally to celebrate. Someone handed Mike a basketball and said, "Let's see you do it again." He let fly from the opposite foul line and swished it!

• • •

So, what's the longest shot in professional basketball?

With just one second remaining on the clock, the Indiana Pacers were trailing the Dallas Chapperals 118–116 in a November 13, 1967 American Basketball Association game. Indiana's Jerry Harkness got the inbounds pass at one end of the court and let fly a stunning ninety-two-foot basket. And since it was a three-point basket, Indiana won the game, 119–118.

"I've been practicing that shot all day," Harkness joked afterwards.

During a February 1992 high school basketball game in Iowa, Waterloo West was trailing 50–49 with one second to go. Scott Ivey took the ball and threw it the length of the court. Nobody caught it. . . . But it bounced off teammate Sean Corbett's head and went right in for the winning basket!

In a December 1992 high school basketball game in Tennessee, York Institute was hosting Livingston Academy. As Livingston charged up the court, they passed the ball ahead to Barry

Webb. The throw was wild and Barry looked like he'd go out of bounds with the ball, so he just threw the ball down on the court as hard as he could. The ball bounced off the court, up into the air . . . and right into the basket for two points.

And it counted! The rules don't say you have to throw the ball into the basket on the fly.

In 1973, fourteen-year-old Craig Schroeder was invited onto center court during the halftime of an NBA game between the Los Angeles Lakers and the Buffalo Braves. As part of the Dodge Colt Shootout, Craig launched a shot that stunned the crowd by going in! For making this forty-seven-foot shot, Craig won a new Dodge Colt—a car he was too young to drive.

In December 1993, Tallahassee Community College was playing Macon College. During the game, thirteen players fouled out or got ejected. Just before halftime, Tallahassee only had four players left. So for more than half the game Macon had five players on the court, while Tallahassee had just four.

And yet Macon still lost, 92–87.

In a December 1990 basketball game in Iowa, the Glidden-Ralston High School team was playing Carroll. But when it came time to start the second half, Carroll's team was still in the locker room.

What to do? The ref handed the ball to Glidden-Ralston, who inbounded. Since they were playing five on none, they scored an easy layup.

Now what to do? Carroll's players were still in the locker room. But it was now their ball.

The referees counted five seconds, called a delay of game violation, and gave the ball back to Glidden-Ralston. They inbounded and scored another easy layup.

At that point Carroll's players came charging onto the floor and rejoined the game.

By the way, this stuff doesn't happen just in high school.

In January 1993, the University of Miami was hosting Pittsburgh. Trailing by two points with eighteen seconds remaining in the game, Pitt called time out under its own basket. When the time-out was over Miami was still in its huddle, so the refs just handed the ball to Pitt. They inbounded and scored an easy two points to tie the game.

At that point Miami came running onto the floor. They inbounded the ball but Pitt stole it and Antoine Jones scored the winning layup with one second left on the clock. That's about as wild an ending as you'll ever see.

Before a November 1994 San Antonio Spurs basketball game at the Alamodome, the Spurs used fireworks as part of the pregame show. There was one problem—the fireworks set off the building's sprinkler system, used to put out fires. Huge torrents of water came shooting out of water cannons into the stands. Fans went scurrying every which way.

Would you believe there was a fifty-minute "rain delay" at an *indoor* basketball game?

In the fall of 1990, prior to the start of the college basketball season, Michigan State was playing an intrasquad game. Right after the opening tip, Matt Stegenga went up for the dunk. He scored, but he also ripped the rim completely off the backboard, causing the glass to shatter. Game cancelled. Final score 2–0.

Said Stegenga, "That's one of the best dunks I've ever had." It certainly was the best dunk of that game!

In December 1992, two Los Angeles Clippers teammates combined on a basket. Loy Vaught picked up Kenny Norman, who then dunked it. It would have been an assist for Vaught, but the NBA does not allow a player to pick up a teammate. No basket!

During an NBA game in March 2001 at the Meadowlands, Stephon Marbury of the New Jersey Nets went in for a "showtime" dunk. He nailed a beautiful windmill jam, but after the ball went through the net, it bounced off Marbury's head and popped back up through the basket and out.

What's the call? The ball had gone through the basket. But it didn't stay through. Sorry, Stephon, no basket!

In January 1960, the Burnsville High School team decided to help senior Danny Heater break the West Virginia state record. At first, Heater wasn't keen on the plan, but after his coach chewed him out, Heater got going. By the third quarter he'd broken the old record of seventy-four points, but the coach kept him in the game.

Burnsville won 173–43, and Heater made fifty-three shots and twenty-nine free throws for a new record of 135 points!

In an NBA game at Madison Square Garden in March 1999, Cleveland Cavaliers coach Mike Fratello called a time out. Nothing unusual about that . . . until Chris Childs, a guard for the New York Knicks, walked over, leaned in, and listened, just as if he played for Cleveland. Well, he wanted to know what the play was going to be! And there's no rule against it.

In April 1999, I saw one of the goofiest basketball plays ever.

There was a jump ball at the foul line in front of the Dallas Mavericks' basket. Chris Mills of the Golden State Warriors got the ball and tried to score a layup, but he was fouled by the Mavericks' Samaki Walker.

What's the problem? Mills was shooting at the wrong basket, and if the ball had gone in it would have counted as two points for Dallas. But he was fouled in the act of shooting.

Can a foul be called when you're shooting at the wrong basket? The refs huddled and ruled no foul. But they did award the ball to Golden State.

In January 1994, the Natrona High School basketball team in Casper, Wyoming, was trailing by one point in the final seconds. So the coach drew up a very simple play—he told Jason Holt to get down on all fours and bark like a dog. Just before his teammate inbounded the ball, Jason "made like Fido" and the other players stopped to look at him. What in the world was he doing? And while Jason was barking his teammate passed the ball to another teammate. Since nobody was playing defense, Natrona got an easy game-winning basket.

Was Jason the hero? Think about it—the coach probably chose the worst shooter to play the part of a dog. Should Jason take that as a compliment?

In February 2003, there was a very close basketball game between Nutley High School and Immaculate Heart Academy in New Jersey. Sarah Clark of Nutley stole an inbounds pass and

dribbled the length of the court for a layup . . . into the wrong basket! That gave Immaculate Heart the lead. But all's well that ends well—Sarah hit the winning foul shots as Nutley won the game 54–53 in two overtimes.

In a December 1997 basketball game near Philadelphia, Penncrest High School took the lead 47–46 with four seconds to go. Strath Haven inbounded the ball, and Bob Kashato took the shot that could win the game. The ball landed on the heel of the rim and just sat there. It didn't move! Time ran out and the game was over. So close and yet . . .

A few years later a similar thing happened in an NBA game. In April 2003, the Los Angeles Clippers were trailing the Memphis Grizzlies by three points with two seconds to play. The Clippers inbounded the ball to Eric Piatkowski, who took a three-point shot for the tie. The ball landed and got wedged between the rim and the backboard. And that's where it was when the buzzer sounded, ending the game.

In an NBA game in December 1991, the Portland Trail Blazers were playing the Denver Nuggets. Coach Rick Adelman of Portland sent Alaa Abdelnaby into the game. He ripped off his warmups and oops . . . he'd forgotten his jersey. He was wearing a tee shirt instead. Abdelnaby had to race off to the locker room to get his uniform!

Coach Adelman was not amused. I don't know if there's any connection, but that was Abdelnaby's last season in Portland.

In January 2004, the Boston Celtics were hosting the Indiana Pacers. As Boston's Paul Pierce cut through the lane, Indiana's Ron Artest tried an interesting defense—he pulled down Pierce's shorts!

Is that legal? The refs either didn't see it or they decided not to call it.

And what about Pierce? He pulled up his shorts, got a pass, and hit a three-point shot!

In April 1995, Brian Williams of the Denver Nuggets caught an alley-oop pass and went to dunk the ball. When his dunk bounced off the rim,

Williams grabbed the rim with his left hand and, while hanging onto the rim, caught the ball with his right. While still hanging there, he dunked the ball.

What's the call? No basket. Williams also received a technical foul for hanging on the rim.

What's the strangest basketball game you ever saw? How about a game where some of the players played for *both* teams in the same game!

This story begins on November 8, 1978. The New Jersey Nets were visiting Philadelphia and the 76ers won in double overtime, 137–133. Or they thought they'd won. . . . During the game a Nets player and his coach were both called for three technical fouls. But you can't be called for three technicals—two is the limit. So the Nets protested, and the game was replayed from the point of the extra technical fouls, with 5:50 left in the third quarter.

Because of scheduling problems, the game couldn't be replayed until March 23, 1979. Meanwhile, four of the players got traded to the other team. The Nets traded Eric Money and another player to the Sixers for Ralph Simpson and Harvey Catchings.

If you look at a box score for this game you'll see that Eric Money, Ralph Simpson, and Harvey Catchings all played for both teams in the same game. But only Eric Money has the distinction of scoring for both teams.

By the way, the Nets finally lost the game, 123–117.

OVERTIME

Shaquille O'Neal's shoe size is 22. The average man's shoe is size 10.

During a 1985 game, Chicago Bulls guard Quintin Dailey ordered a pizza, which he ate on the bench at the end of the third quarter.

In a game for the New York Knicks, Latrell Sprewell once made a basket while sitting on the floor!

In a 1969 Tennessee girl's high school basketball game, Chattanooga East Ridge defeated Ooltewah 38–37 in a record *sixteen* overtimes.

The shortest player in the NBA was "Muggsy" Bogues at 5 feet, 3 inches. And the winner of the 1986 NBA All-Star Slam Dunk contest was 5-foot-7-inch "Spud" Webb.

The 1981–82 Denver Nuggets are the only NBA team to go an entire season scoring over 100 points or more in every game. They are also the only team to allow 100 points or more in every game. Their record that year was 46 wins, 36 losses.

In Colorado, Las Animas High School defeated La Junta, 2–0, and that game had to go into overtime!

The Los Angeles Lakers won a record 33 games in a row at the start of the 1971–72 season.

During all 79 games of the 1961–62 season, Wilt Chamberlain played every minute of every game.

HOCKEY

As you've probably heard, this sport was invented in Canada. Lacrosse players flattened their round ball, altered the stick a bit, found a frozen lake, and laced up some skates. Yeah, that's the story. Or is it?

It turns out that they played some form of hockey in England in the 1500s, around the time of Queen Elizabeth and the defeat of the Spanish Armada! Would you believe the British banned the game because it was too violent? Hmmm.

There's no question about it—hockey is not for the timid, no matter when or where it's played. After all, players are flying around a slippery surface with razor blades attached to their feet. And they slam into their opponents at full speed, knocking them into what people still call the "boards" even though half of them are now made out of glass.

Some call hockey the fastest game in the world. Maybe that explains why the puck can take some pretty strange bounces. I've seen goaltenders score goals. I've seen a puck go into the net off a player's rear end. One guy shot the puck so hard that it hit the glass and disintegrated. Not the glass—the puck!

And then there are the fights—I've seen goalies fight, coaches fight, and even brothers on opposite teams fight!

So, get ready for the face-off, the puck is about to drop for some wacky hockey moments.

During a February 2004 NHL hockey game, a major brawl broke out on the ice. And then something happened that you don't normally see. The two goaltenders—Ty Conklin for the Edmonton Oilers and Pasi Nurminen for the Atlanta Thrashers—wearing their full gear, started fighting with each other, right in the middle of the rink.

Eventually, things settled down. But after the refs handed out penalties Atlanta lost Nurminen for the rest of the game. And since their backup goalie had been injured earlier, Atlanta had to play the last 1:49 without a goalie!

Kind of made it easy for Edmonton to score, don't you think? In fact, Edmonton did score a goal.

Most hockey fans like to see high-scoring games. Get rid of goalies—that'll do it!

In January 1996, Todd Bertuzzi was playing left wing for the New York Islanders against the Montreal Canadiens. The puck was loose behind the goal, and as it rolled along the ice, Bertuzzi just picked up the back of the net and let the puck trickle in.

Was it a goal? Well, the puck was in the net . . . but you have to score a goal from in front of the net. So no, it didn't count.

A few years later, Bertuzzi was playing for the Vancouver Canucks. In a November 2000 game against the Colorado Rockies he had his stick knocked from his hands by a defenseman. So Todd began to "stickhandle" the puck with his feet. He skated the puck from one foot to the other and then kicked the puck into the goal!

No, that didn't count either.

When the ref lost sight of the puck during a January 2003 game between the Toronto Maple Leafs and the Calgary Flames he blew his whistle, stopping play. But where was it? Nowhere on the ice. Turns out it had landed in Shayne Corson's shorts.

Corson skated around, grabbing between his legs for the puck, but he couldn't reach it. Finally, the linesman skated over to him, reached into Corson's shorts from behind and, to the cheers of the crowd, he pulled out the puck!

When the Boston Bruins hosted the Detroit Red Wings on November 10, 1948, the game had to be stopped just nine minutes after it began. The problem was *fog*!

The inside of the Boston Garden was so humid that a thick fog made it impossible for the players to see. The game was rescheduled for the next day.

During the playoffs, NHL games can't end in a tie, so the teams have to keep playing until there is a winner. The longest playoff game ever began on March 24, 1936 and ended on the 25th!

The Detroit Red Wings and Montreal Maroons were deadlocked at 0–0 at the end of regulation time. They played one overtime period. Then a second. Then a third. A fourth. A fifth. Finally, at

2:25 am the next day, this marathon game ended when Detroit's "Mud" Bruneteau scored the game's only goal in the seventeenth minute of the sixth overtime period after two hours, fifty-six minutes, and thirty seconds of play. That's almost a triple-header!

The game took five hours and fifty-one minutes from the opening face-off. Detroit goalie Norm Smith turned aside 92 shots, an NHL record for the longest shutout.

How quickly can two teams score hockey goals? On December 19, 1987, the St. Louis Blues were visiting the Boston Bruins. Late in the game, Ken Linesman of Boston scored a goal. Just *two* seconds later, Doug Gilmour scored for St. Louis. Two goals in two seconds. And yes, that's a record!

On Valentine's Day 1996, the Indianapolis Ice minor league team decided to have their players wear pink jerseys with nice big hearts on the backs and sleeves. It was a rare Central Hockey League game without a single fight.

Apparently love does conquer all!

In April 1997 the Hartford Whalers were playing the Buffalo Sabres. Keith Primeau played for Hartford, and his younger brother Wayne played for Buffalo. It was the first time they'd shared the ice in the same NHL game. And wouldn't you know it, during the game the two of them got into an all-out brawl.

My guess is this argument probably began when they were a lot younger.

In November 1990, the Edmonton Oilers were hosting the Vancouver Canucks. At one point a fight broke out involving most of the players on the ice. All except for three Edmonton players. So they just took the puck and passed it down the ice, and Craig Simpson beat the Vancouver goalie for a goal.

Makes it kind of easy when there is no defense!

OVERTIME

Toronto Maple Leaf Gus Bodnar scored a goal fifteen seconds into the first period of his first NHL game, October 30, 1943.

Bill Mosienko of the Chicago Black Hawks scored three goals in just twenty-one seconds against the New York Rangers on March 23, 1952. By coincidence, Gus Bodnar, then playing for Chicago, assisted on all three goals.

During his seven seasons from 1955–56 to 1961–62, goalies Glenn Hall played 4,200 minutes—that's every minute of every game.

When Calgary crushed the San Jose Sharks 13–1 on February 10, 1993, the Flames goalie Jeff Reese had three assists—an NHL record for a goalie.

Theo Fleury got blood on his hockey jersey during a game and the team didn't have a spare. So Theo put on a fan's jersey that said FLEURY on the back!

GOLF

Some people say that golf is the hardest individual sport to master. But think about that for a moment. Golf is the only sport where the ball doesn't move when play begins. And there's nobody playing defense. Heck, people aren't allowed to even make noise while you're playing.

In baseball, a rock-hard ball is coming at your head at 100 miles per hour, fans are shouting obscenities at you, and you're supposed to be as cool as a cucumber. In golf, it's as if you're playing in a library. Golfers have gone nuts if they've heard as much as a camera click.

And boy, that ball takes some strange bounces!

I've seen a shot bounce off a tree and into the cup for a hole in one. I saw a ball take one bounce and go into a trash can. Balls have even landed in a person's lap.

One time Tiger Woods was putting and the ball was going right at the hole when it hit a bee that had landed on the green—the ball veered away and missed the cup!

I've seen golf balls hit squirrels. I saw one hit a bird in midflight. I've also seen a bird swoop down onto the course, pick up a ball in its beak, and drop the ball in a nearby lake.

So let's "tee it up" and discover some of golf's funniest bloopers. Laughter is par for this course.

In May 1998, Todd Obuchowski was playing golf at the Beaver Brook Golf Course in Haydenville, Massachusetts. The 116-yard fourth hole at Beaver Brook runs along a highway. Unfortunately, Todd hit his shot directly onto the road.

Fortunately for him, that was where Nancy Bachan was driving her Toyota at about thirty miles per hour. The ball bounced off her car, ricocheted onto the green, and went into the cup for a hole in one!

Unfortunately for Nancy, the dent in her car cost $150 to repair. But fortunately for her, Todd's amazing shot quickly turned him into a minor celebrity. He appeared on *The Tonight Show,* where host Jay Leno gave him a check to pay for Nancy's repairs.

81

For most golfers, a hole in one is a once-in-a-lifetime event. Not for Jim Cobb. On August 4, 1985, he aced the 167-yard 7th hole at the Meeker Golf Course in Colorado. The next day he did the same thing on the 3rd hole at the nearby Yampa Valley course. And then Cobb did it *again*—his tee-shot on the 162-yard 9th hole rolled in. That's three holes in one in just two days!

At the January 2002 South African PGA Championship in Johannesburg, James Kingston teed off on the fifteenth hole. An ace would win him a new Audi, but Kingston's tee shot was terrible. He hooked it to the left and the ball went straight for the trees. After the ball crashed into some branches it made a hard right turn onto the green . . . and trickled into the cup for an amazing, car-winning, hole-in-one!

In March 1990, Dale Eggeling was playing on the LPGA tour in Florida. Her tee shot took a big bounce and landed right in the lap of a guy sitting in a golf cart. In golf, the rule is that you have to hit the ball where it lies.

Dale walked over, found her ball in the guy's lap and started waving both hands, shouting, "I'm not touching that!"

Luckily for the guy, Eggerling was allowed a free drop without a penalty.

In July 1990, Chi Chi Rodriguez chipped the ball onto the green and a dog ran up, took the ball in his mouth, and ran off.

How do you score it? A birdie? An eagle? No, a *beagle!*

Actually, Chi Chi got a free drop on the green.

In April 1997, Scott Hoch was putting on the eighteenth green during the Players Championship in Florida. After he hit the ball a fan ran right through the green between Hoch and his rolling ball—without affecting the putt—then dove into the pond next to the green.

Said one TV commentator. "Why is it you can never find a good alligator when you need one!"

In November 2002, golfer Eduardo Romero was playing in the Warburg Cup on St. Simon's Island, Georgia. On the seventh hole, his approach shot landed on the green about twenty feet from the hole. It was very windy that day, and Romero's putt was directly into the wind. He stroked the ball, but it stopped about three feet shy of the hole. And before Romero could reach his ball, the wind blew it backwards and clear off the green!

In January 2000, it hailed during the Williams World Challenge in Scottsdale, Arizona. No, not hail the size of golf balls . . . smaller. Still, hail covered everything, so the officials announced a one-hour delay to clear the ice off the greens. But Phil Mickelson, who was on one of the greens, decided to chip instead of putt from about twelve feet away. And he chipped it in for a birdie!

There's no rule that says you have to putt a ball on the green.

At the 2000 U.S. Open at Pebble Beach, California, one of Angel Cabrera's tee shots took one bounce and landed in a garbage can. Did Angel have to hit the ball where it was? The rules say a garbage can is a movable obstruction. Cabrera did not have to play the ball where it lay. He was allowed to lift—and, more importantly,

clean the ball—before dropping it next to the can.

The "garbage-can-in-one" was probably the most memorable moment of Cabrera's U.S. Open that year. He finished with a score of 298 and earned $22,000. That was twenty-six shots and $778,000 behind the winner, Tiger Woods.

In August 1995, 102-year-old Harley Potter from Winston-Salem, North Carolina, played in the Over 100 Golf Championship. Harley shot a 160 the first day, 180 the next—and he won! Harley had an excuse for his high scores—he was a new golfer. "I started when I was 92, and I never had a lesson!"

At the New Orleans Open golf tournament in April 1990, Mike Sullivan was having a problem on a par-3 water hole. The ball was right up against a wooden railing and Mike had to balance himself on top of the railing to try to chip the ball up onto the green. He kept chopping at the ball and it wouldn't budge. He tried a fourth shot. Then a fifth. Then a sixth. Finally, his next shot actually got the ball in the air, but when it hit the ground

the ball hopped backwards into the lake! We're still doing the math. We think Mike shot an 11 on this par 3!

Worst score during a major golf tournament? Roy Ainsley took 19 strokes at the par-4 sixteenth hole at the 1938 U.S. Open. He took most of them while attempting to hit a ball out of a brook.

The city of Socorro, New Mexico holds an annual golf tournament called Elfego Baca Shoot. The course is only one hole—five miles down a mountain, through lots of boulders and cactus. This one hole is a par-50 and takes about five hours to play. The winner in 2000 scored a 36, which included penalties for eight lost balls!

What's the longest golf drive ever?

In September 1990, Kelly Murray drove a golf ball a record 684.8 yards. Turns out Murray was standing on top of a platform at an airport in British Columbia, and he drove the ball down the runway! The ball kept bouncing, and bouncing, and bouncing. . . .

Hey, it was still a record—nobody said it had to be on grass!

In April 1995, they shut down a runway at the Philadelphia airport so that Laura Davies could drive a golf ball down that tarmac. Her distance? A women's world driving record, 376 yards.

At the Players Championship in March 1999, Freddy Couples stepped up to the tee on the famed seventeenth hole at Sawgrass, a par-3 island green. Couples knocked his shot right into the water. So, after taking his penalty, he hit another ball. And the ball went into the hole on a fly!

If it was his first shot, it would have been a hole in one. But because of the penalty, Couples scored a 3, which is par for that hole.

SUDDEN DEATH

The world's longest hole in golf is the 7th at the Satsuki Golf Club in Japan—a 909 yard par seven. The shortest championship hole is the 7th at Pebble Beach, California—it's just 106 yards.

The longest unofficial golf "course" was the entire United States. From September 14, 1963 to October 3, 1964, golfer Floyd Satterlee Rood played coast-to-coast— from the Pacific Ocean to the Atlantic—in a total of 114,737 strokes. During that time he lost 3,511 balls over the 3,398 miles.

Scott Palmer made a hole in one in each of four consecutive rounds from October 9–12, 1983, at Balboa Park in San Diego. Palmer also holds the record for most aces in one year—33, from June 5, 1983 to May 31, 1984. Not surprisingly, Palmer also holds the record for most holes in one in a career—100.

Four golfers at the U.S. Open all hit holes in one on the same day—June 16, 1989. Jerry Pate, Nick Price, Doug Weaver, and Mark Weibe all aced the 167-yard par-3 sixth hole at Oak Hill Country Club in Rochester, NY.

Who's the oldest player to hit a hole in one? Harold Stilson of Deerfield Beach, Florida, was 101 years old when he got his ace. And the youngest ever to hit a hole in one— Jake Paine of California, was 3 years old when he holed his tee shot!

At a charity golf tournament in Barrington, Rhode Island, on the same hole, on consecutive swings, golfers Lee Jantzen and Scott McCarron both had holes in one.

In July 1999, in Milwaukee, a golfer named Worth Dalton had a hole in one. Dalton is blind.

TENNIS

Men and women chasing tennis balls around the court at high speed can produce some pretty unusual bounces.

I've seen shots hit the linesmen, the ball boys, and even the umpires! I've seen a ball in play hit a bird in mid flight. I've also seen partners in doubles run after the ball, collide with each other, and fall to the ground.

And tennis has some pretty weird rules. For example, you don't have to hit the ball over the net. You can hit around the net as long as the ball goes into the court on the other side.

I've seen players hit serves 150 miles per hour. And I've seen players hit underhanded serves at 30 miles per hour—a little kid could return that!

And then there are the fans. . . . When players serve, the fans are supposed to be quiet and not move. But for some reason, fans seem to make noise at the absolute worst moments. I've heard cell phones go off during serves.

Once, when John McEnroe was about to serve, a couple was having a loud conversation behind him. He just stopped in the middle of his serve, turned around, and yelled, "Do you mind?!"

In case you don't remember, John McEnroe was the famous bad boy of tennis. He ranted and raved at umpires. He virtually invented the phrase "You can't be serious," which he screamed at one umpire after a call he didn't agree with.

So get ready to receive as we serve up some wild and weird tennis moments.

In August 1999, Pete Sampras served the ball and it went right through Patrick Rafter's racket, breaking the strings. Now that's a hard serve!

In November 2000, Goran Ivanisevic was playing tennis against Hyung-Taik Lee of Korea. Ivanisevic was having a very tough day. Nothing was going his way—his serve was terrible and so were his forehand, his backhand, and his volley. And as things went from bad to worse he slammed his rackets to the ground in frustration, breaking them one by one. Finally, by the third

set he'd tossed his last racket into a garbage can. He had no rackets left, so he had to forfeit the match!

In March 1994, Boris Becker was playing Andre Agassi in a tennis tournament in Miami. Becker couldn't seem to return anything Agassi hit that day, so in a fit of desperation he walked over to one of the ball girls, gave her his racquet, and said, "You give it a go." To the crowd's delight, the ball girl walked onto the court and rallied with Agassi.

At the 2004 French Open, there was a tennis match that didn't want to end. In the first round they played tiebreakers in the first four sets, but not in the deciding fifth. So the fifth set between Fabrice Santoro and Arnaud Clément just kept going and going and going . . .

Finally, Santoro beat Clément 4–6, 3–6, 7–6, 6–3, 16–14. The match took six hours and thirty-three minutes—the longest recorded tennis match. In fact, it took two days to play the match because darkness forced them to stop before it was completed, and they had to finish the next day.

Compare that with the 1926 women's final, also at the French Open. Suzanne Lenglen beat Mary K. Browne, 5–1, 6–0, in just twenty-seven minutes.

What was the longest single point in tennis? In October 1984, Jean Hepner was playing Vicky Nelson in Richmond, Virginia. The ball went back and forth over the net 643 times!

That one point lasted twenty-nine minutes— two minutes *longer* than the entire 1926 French Open women's final.

Jimmy Connors made two amazing shots. One counted, but the other didn't.

During one point, Jimmy threw his tennis racquet into the air. The ball hit his racquet and bounced into his opponent's court, and the stunned player couldn't return it.

Another time, at the U.S. Open, Connors hit a shot around the net and into the court on the other side. The ball never went over the net.

The one that counts? The "around the net" shot. There's no rule that says you have to hit it over the net, you just have to hit it into the court on the other side, no matter how it gets there.

Unfortunately for Jimmy, a player has to be holding his racquet when he returns the ball. The ball off his airborne racquet didn't count.

During a doubles match at the January 2002 Australian Open, a bird flew across the court just above the net, chasing a moth. Bad idea. A forehand

smash by Michael Llodra of France nailed the bird, and it dropped like a rock to the court. Julien Boutter, another Frenchman, raced over to the bird, which was lying motionless on the court. Boutter got down on his knees, put his palms together, crossed himself, and said a little prayer for the bird.

Sad to say, his prayer wasn't answered. It was a bad day all around for Boutter. He lost the match as well.

What's the ultimate sports fantasy? You go to a game as a fan and become the hero!

John Pius Boland was a student at Oxford University in England. He became friends with Thrasyvoalos Manaos, a student from Greece, and accepted an invitation to visit Athens during the 1896 Easter holidays, which was also when the Olympic Games were to be held. While Boland was there he played some friendly games of tennis with Manaos, who happened to be a member of the Greek Olympic Committee. Manaos was impressed with Boland's play and entered him in the Olympics.

To everyone's surprise, John Pius Boland won two gold medals, for both singles and doubles!

At the 1993 Wimbledon tournament, Natasha Zvereva was teamed in doubles with Gigi Fernandez. During one match, Natasha slipped while hitting an overhead and fell to her knees. As luck would have it, the return came to Natasha and she hit the ball back while still kneeling on the ground. And, would you believe it . . . while she was still on the ground the ball came back to her *again*, and she successfully hit it a second time over the net!

Natasha then got up and the ball came to her yet again. She proceeded to hit a weak overhead, but one of her opponents hit it into the net.

Zvereva and Fernandez won one of the most amazing points in women's tennis. They also won the championship that year in doubles and the French and Australian Open doubles championships as well. Not a bad year!

TIEBREAKER

A 1955 Wimbledon finalist, Beverly Baker Fleitz, switched her racket from one hand to the other so that she only hit the ball forehand — she had no backhand!

One of the longest tennis points ever played took 51 1/2 minutes. It was a match between two eleven-year-olds at the 1977 Anaheim, California, junior championships.

At the start of her first match at Wimbledon, Maria de Amorin served seventeen double faults in a row.

A MIXED BAG

What about all those events that don't fit into the category of major sports? I'm talking about the Thumb Wrestling Championship. That really exists. So does the Shin-Kicking Championship. And there's also a Rock Paper Scissors Championship.

Then there are those wacky races. How about a horse race with only one horse in the race? That really happened. In another race, a horse crosses the finish line first but he didn't win—you'll have to read this chapter to find out why.

Of course, horses aren't the only animals that race. You've probably heard of dog racing, but I've also seen sheep race. And pigs. I've even seen rats racing! Since they call the Kentucky Derby the "Run for the Roses," I suppose that has to be the "Run for the Rodents!"

And what's with all the fights? Sure, they're supposed to fight in boxing and you've probably seen it in baseball . . . but in car racing? I've seen drivers mix it up. Talk about road rage!

I've also seen a marathon race where two runners stopped and started a fistfight right in the middle of the street. Get those guys some boxing gloves!

All kinds of strange stuff happens in sports. And that means all sorts of goofy stuff happens as well. We're calling this group of oddball stories a mixed bag, and boy, is it ever mixed up!

Did you hear about the Australian swimming coach who had a unique training tool? As the members of his team jumped into the pool, the coach threw a live crocodile into the water to chase the swimmers. It somehow made them go just a bit faster. . . .

At a January 1997 horse race in Australia, a pack of horses was heading for the finish line when one of them stumbled and created a chain-reaction accident. As the other horses started to go down, one quick-thinking jockey jumped off his stumbling mount and right into the saddle of another horse who had thrown his jockey.

This jockey finished the race on a different horse than the one he started on. And while you have to admire his creativity, that's against the rules.

In April 1994 at Yonkers Raceway, New York, they ran a race with only one horse. Wizard of Hearts was his name—and he won!

First prize was $20,000 dollars. That was $20,000 more than any of the bettors won: the Raceway didn't allow betting on this one-horse race.

Three years later, at Hollywood Park in California, a filly named Sharp Cat was the only horse in a race, and she also won. All she had to do was finish the race and the owners would pocket $60,000. She did and they did.

These one-horse races—called walkovers— happen when all the other horses in a race drop out at the last minute, mostly because of injuries or problems with their jockeys.

In September 2000 at Santa Anita Raceway in California, jockey Kent Desormeaux was aboard a horse named Lido. The horse finished first, but he lost the race.

It seems that just as he got to the finish line, Lido veered off to the right, throwing Desormeaux inches before the end of the race. So Lido was disqualified for not crossing the finish line carrying his required weight!

Did you hear the one about the jockey who rode a horse and an SUV in the same race? In January 2002, there was a steeplechase horse race in Southwell, England. All seven entries in the race fell down, including Tony McCoy aboard the favorite, a horse named Family Business.

McCoy had fallen early in the race and was headed back to the jockey room. But after he saw that all the horses had fallen, McCoy got a lift in a Land Rover and was driven back to his horse. He completed the race ten minutes and thirty seconds after it began. That's about four minutes longer than a normal race, but it was all perfectly legal.

In March 1996, there was a major snowstorm in Buffalo, New York. But that didn't stop the local track from running the races. Of course, nobody could see anything—not the fans, not the TV cameras, and not the race announcer.

I loved this call by Peter Szymanski: "Into the far turn . . . Hello . . . Horsies . . . where are you?"

The year before, at the same Buffalo Raceway, there was a horse race in the fog. Again, Syzmanski was at his best. At one point he screamed into the microphone "I hear hoofbeats, but I can't see 'em!"

And in June 1989, there was a horse race at Monmouth Park in New Jersey. Once more, there was a heavy fog and no one could see a thing. But that didn't stop the track from running the first race. Here's what the announcer said: "They race past the stands into the first turn with Hot Lights Excellence in front. On the outside, Equal to None is second as they disappear into the fog. . . . From now on, you're on your own!"

Did you hear about the fan at an October 1997 Spanish bullfight who ran into the arena to join the action? The bull's horns caught the guy's leg, and the bull tossed him up in the air and onto the ground. Somehow, a horn slid inside the man's pants and when the bull flipped the guy

over, his pants came off. He was "de-pantsed" by the bull!

Fortunately, the spectator wasn't hurt. He was last seen running out of the arena pulling his shirt down as low as it could go to cover up his embarrassment. As for the bull, he stood quietly off to the side with remnants of the guy's underpants dangling from his horns. Now that's a major-league wedgie.

In October 1989, English boxer Tony Wilson was losing his fight with Steve McCarthy when Tony's mother, Minna, climbed into the ring and beat McCarthy over the head with her shoe, opening a cut on Steve's head. The injured boxer had to leave the ring to get four stitches. Afterward, he refused to continue the fight, so Wilson was declared the winner!

In an April 1990 Golden Gloves boxing match at Madison Square Garden in New York, Gene Van Oss was fighting Patrick Shea. Both fighters swung simultaneously. Both connected. And both fighters went down. It was a double knockdown.

What's the rule? Van Oss got up, so he won. If neither man had stood back up, the match would have been declared a draw.

During an October 1997 cross-country bicycle race in Brazil, the riders had to go over a small bridge. One rider looked back to see who was gaining on him . . . veered slightly off the road . . . and missed the bridge. He and his bike went over a small railing and dove right into the river!

Luckily, it wasn't a high bridge or a big river. The rider was muddied and embarrassed, but unhurt.

In a March 1990 boxing match, fighter Bazooka Limon was having no success against Sharmba Mitchell. So, in an act of desperation, he pulled down Mitchell's shorts!

Pulling down an opponent's shorts isn't allowed, but the next time Mitchell fought he came into the ring wearing a pair of suspenders.

In another boxing match in March 1990, the two fighters were in the corner. Vincent Pettway swung but missed his opponent. The punch caught referee Frank Cappacino right in the face.

It's not often that you see the referee get knocked out!

At the July 1981 National Sports Festival in Syracuse, New York, two-time All-Around Champion Big Ten gymnast Brian Meeker was ready to begin his vault. The idea in vaulting is to run as fast as you can, put your hands on the vault, and jump over it. But on this day, running at full speed, Meeker didn't go over the vault—he ran smack into it!

Meeker wasn't hurt, but he was embarrassed. More people know him for that mishap than all of his many other accomplishments. Several years later, I gave him another chance on "Spanning the World." He easily cleared the vault, and as he flew over the vault in slow-motion we played the music from the "Hallelujah Chorus."

MORE FOR THE MIX

In Chico, California, a dog named Tabiah averaged 57 in bowling league play.

The closest finish in Grand Prix auto racing was when Ayrton Senna defeated Nigel Mansell in the 1986 Spanish Grand Prix by 0.014 seconds.

In a 1909 fight in Paris, heavyweight Joe Jeannette was knocked down 27 times but still beat Sam McVey in the 49th round.

The winner of the 1898 Boston Marathon was named Ronald McDonald.

What are the odds? In a horse race with eight horses in the field, the #1 horse finished first, the #2 horse finished second, the #3 was third . . . right on through to #8, who finished last.

SO LET'S SUM UP.

We've had a basketball player bark like a dog; we've had a golf shot bounce off a moving car and into the hole for a hole in one; we've had a baseball player throw a potato instead of a baseball, and we've had a boxer's mom rush into the ring to beat up her son's opponent. In short, you just can't make this stuff up. I think the reason we love sports is that it's so unpredictable. Anything can happen . . . and it usually does. And I'm convinced that wacky stories like these make us love sports even more. So let's make a deal: You keep enjoying sports, and I'll keep collecting these crazy stories. And maybe we'll talk again sometime.

One more thing—it's my sincere hope that after you play sports you can tell a great story ending with, "AND NOBODY GOT HURT!"

Emmy Award–winning sportscaster LEN BERMAN has been collecting weird and wacky sports stories to show on his TV segment "Spanning the World" for more than twenty years. A regular on NBC's *Today Show,* Len is a six-time winner of the Sportscaster of the Year Award given by the National Sportscasters and Sportswriters Association, and he has reported on major sports events around the globe, including multiple Olympic Games.

KENT GAMBLE has been a freelance illustrator since 1977. His work has appeared in the *New York Times, People, Golf Digest, Marvel Comics,* and many other periodicals. He has illustrated three humorous books published by Texas Tech University Press, as well as the children's book *Look Who's Going to Texas Tech,* by Marsha Gustafson. He lives in Lubbock, Texas.